PRAISE OF FOLLY

By ERASMUS

Translated by JOHN WILSON

Praise of Folly
By Erasmus
Translated by John Wilson

Print ISBN 13: 978-1-4209-6181-2
eBook ISBN 13: 978-1-4209-6182-9

This edition copyright © 2019. Digireads.com Publishing.

Cover Image: a detail of a portrait of Erasmus of Rotterdam Writing, c. 1523 (mixed technique on paper, mounted on fir wood), by Hans Holbein the Younger (1497/8-1543) / Kunstmuseum, Basel, Switzerland / Bridgeman Images.

Please visit *www.digireads.com*

ERASMUS OF ROTTERDAM

To his friend

THOMAS MORE, health:

As I was coming awhile since out of Italy for England, that I might not waste all that time I was to sit on horseback in foolish and illiterate fables, I chose rather one while to revolve with myself something of our common studies, and other while to enjoy the remembrance of my friends, of whom I left here some no less learned than pleasant. Among these you, my More, came first in my mind, whose memory, though absent yourself, gives me such delight in my absence, as when present with you I ever found in your company; than which, let me perish if in all my life I ever met with anything more delectable. And therefore, being satisfied that something was to be done, and that that time was no wise proper for any serious matter, I resolved to make some sport with the praise of folly. But who the devil put that in your head? you'll say. The first thing was your surname of More, which comes so near the word *Moriae* (folly) as you are far from the thing. And that you are so, all the world will clear you. In the next place, I conceived this exercise of wit would not be least approved by you; inasmuch as you are wont to be delighted with such kind of mirth, that is to say, neither unlearned, if I am not mistaken, nor altogether insipid, and in the whole course of your life have played the part of a Democritus. And though such is the excellence of your judgment that it was ever contrary to that of the people's, yet such is your incredible affability and sweetness of temper that you both can and delight to carry yourself to all men a man of all hours. Wherefore you will not only with good will accept this small declamation, but take upon you the defense of it, for as much as being dedicated to you, it is now no longer mine but yours. But perhaps there will not be wanting some wranglers that may cavil and charge me, partly that these toys are lighter than may become a divine, and partly more biting than may beseem the modesty of a Christian, and consequently exclaim that I resemble the ancient comedy, or another Lucian, and snarl at everything. But I would have them whom the lightness or foolery of the argument may offend to consider that mine is not the first of this kind, but the same thing that has been often practiced even by great authors: when Homer, so many ages since, did the like with the battle of frogs and mice; Virgil, with the gnat and puddings; Ovid, with the nut; when Polycrates and his corrector Isocrates extolled tyranny; Glauco, injustice; Favorinus, deformity and the quartan ague; Synescius, baldness; Lucian, the fly and flattery; when Seneca made such sport with Claudius' canonizations; Plutarch, with his dialogue between Ulysses and Gryllus; Lucian and Apuleius, with the ass; and some other, I know not who, with the hog that made his last will and testament, of which also even St. Jerome makes mention. And therefore if they please, let them suppose I played at tables for my diversion, or if they had rather have it so, that I rode on a hobbyhorse. For what injustice is it that when we allow every course of life its recreation, that study only should have none? Especially when such toys are not without their serious matter, and foolery is so handled that the reader that is not altogether thick-skulled may reap more benefit from it than from some men's crabbish and specious arguments. As when one, with long study and great pains, patches many pieces together on the praise of rhetoric or philosophy; another makes a panegyric to a prince; another encourages him to a war against the Turks; another tells you what will become of the world after himself is dead; and another finds out some new device for the better ordering of goat's wool: for as nothing is more trifling than to treat of serious matters triflingly, so nothing carries a better grace than so to discourse of trifles as a man may seem to have intended them least. For my own part, let other men judge of what I have written; though yet, unless an overweening opinion of myself may have made me blind in my own cause, I have praised folly, but not altogether foolishly. And now to say somewhat to that other cavil, of biting. This liberty was ever permitted to all men's wits, to make their smart, witty reflections on the common errors of mankind, and that too without offense, as long as this liberty does not run into licentiousness; which makes me the more admire the tender ears of the men of this age, that can away with solemn titles. No, you'll meet with some so preposterously religious that they will sooner endure the broadest scoffs even against Christ himself than hear the Pope or a prince be touched in the least, especially if it be anything that concerns their profit; whereas he that so taxes the lives of men, without naming anyone in particular, whither, I pray, may he be said to bite, or rather to teach and admonish? Or otherwise, I beseech you, under how many notions do I tax myself? Besides, he that spares no sort of men cannot be said to be angry with anyone in particular, but the vices of all. And therefore, if there shall happen to be anyone that shall say he is hit, he will but discover either his guilt or fear. Saint Jerome sported in this kind with more freedom and greater sharpness, not sparing sometimes men's very name. But I, besides that I have wholly avoided it, I have so moderated my style that the understanding reader will easily perceive my endeavors herein were rather to make mirth than bite. Nor have I, after the example of Juvenal, raked up that forgotten sink of filth and ribaldry, but laid before you things rather ridiculous than dishonest. And now, if there be anyone that is yet dissatisfied, let him at least remember that it is no dishonor to be discommended by Folly; and having brought her in speaking, it was but fit that I kept up the character of the person. But why do I run over these things to you, a person so excellent an advocate that no man better defends his client, though the cause many times be none of the best? Farewell, my best disputant More, and stoutly defend your *Moriae*.

From the country,
the 5th of the Ides of June.

PRAISE OF FOLLY

An oration, of feigned matter, spoken
by Folly in her own person

At what rate soever the world talks of me (for I am not ignorant what an ill report Folly has got, even among the most foolish), yet that I am that she, that only she, whose deity recreates both gods and men, even this is a sufficient argument, that I no sooner stepped up to speak to this full assembly than all your faces put on a kind of new and unwonted pleasantness. So suddenly have you cleared your brows, and with so frolic and hearty a laughter given me your applause, that in truth as many of you as I behold on every side of me seem to me no less than Homer's gods drunk with nectar and nepenthe; whereas before, you sat as lumpish and pensive as if you had come from consulting an oracle. And as it usually happens when the sun begins to show his beams, or when after a sharp winter the spring breathes afresh on the earth, all things immediately get a new face, new color, and recover as it were a certain kind of youth again: in like manner, by but beholding me you have in an instant gotten another kind of countenance; and so what the otherwise great rhetoricians with their tedious and long-studied orations can hardly effect, to wit, to remove the trouble of the mind, I have done it at once with my single look.

But if you ask me why I appear before you in this strange dress, be pleased to lend me your ears, and I'll tell you; not those ears, I mean, you carry to church, but abroad with you, such as you are wont to prick up to jugglers, fools, and buffoons, and such as our friend Midas once gave to Pan. For I am disposed awhile to play the sophist with you; not of their sort who nowadays boozle young men's heads with certain empty notions and curious trifles, yet teach them nothing but a more than womanish obstinacy of scolding: but I'll imitate those ancients who, that they might the better avoid that infamous appellation of *sophi* or *wise*, chose rather to be called sophists. Their business was to celebrate the praises of the gods and valiant men. And the like encomium shall you hear from me, but neither of Hercules nor Solon, but my own dear self, that is to say, Folly. Nor do I esteem a rush that call it a foolish and insolent thing to praise one's self. Be it as foolish as they would make it, so they confess it proper: and what can be more than that Folly be her own trumpet? For who can set me out better than myself, unless perhaps I could be better known to another than to myself? Though yet I think it somewhat more modest than the general practice of our nobles and wise men who, throwing away all shame, hire some flattering orator or lying poet from whose mouth they may hear their praises, that is to say, mere lies; and yet, composing themselves with a seeming modesty, spread out their peacock's plumes and erect their crests, while this impudent flatterer equals a man of nothing to the gods and proposes him as an absolute pattern of all virtue that's wholly a stranger to it, sets out a pitiful jay in other's feathers, washes the Blackmoor white, and lastly swells a gnat to an elephant. In short, I will follow that old proverb that says, "He may lawfully praise himself that lives far from neighbors." Though, by the way, I cannot but wonder at the ingratitude, shall I say, or negligence of men who, notwithstanding they honor me in the first place and are willing enough to confess my bounty, yet not one of them for these so many ages has there been who in some thankful oration has set out the praises of Folly; when yet there has not wanted them whose elaborate endeavors have extolled tyrants, agues, flies, baldness, and such other pests of nature, to their own loss of both time and sleep. And now you shall hear from me a plain extemporary speech, but so much the truer. Nor would I have you think it like the rest of orators, made for the ostentation of wit; for these, as you know, when they have been beating their heads some thirty years about an oration and at last perhaps produce somewhat that was never their own, shall yet swear they composed it in three days, and that too for diversion: whereas I ever liked it best to speak whatever came first out.

But let none of you expect from me that after the manner of rhetoricians I should go about to define what I am, much less use any division; for I hold it equally unlucky to circumscribe her whose deity is universal, or make the least division in that worship about which everything is so generally agreed. Or to what purpose, think you, should I describe myself when I am here present before you, and you behold me speaking? For I am, as you see, that true and only giver of wealth whom the Greeks call Μωρία, the Latins *Stultitia*, and our plain English *Folly*. Or what need was there to have said so much, as if my very looks were not sufficient to inform you who I am? Or as if any man, mistaking me for wisdom, could not at first sight convince himself by my face the true index of my mind? I am no counterfeit, nor do I carry one thing in my looks and another in my breast. No, I am in every respect so like myself that neither can they dissemble me who arrogate to themselves the appearance and title of wise men and walk like asses in scarlet hoods, though after all their hypocrisy Midas' ears will discover their master. A most ungrateful generation of men that, when they are wholly given up to my party, are yet publicly ashamed of the name, as taking it for a reproach; for which cause, since in truth they are Μωρότατοι, fools, and yet would appear to the world to be wise men and Thales, we'll even call them Μωροσόφους, wise fools.

Nor will it be amiss also to imitate the rhetoricians of our times, who think themselves in a manner gods if like horse leeches they can but appear to be double-tongued, and believe they have done a mighty act if in their Latin orations they can but shuffle in some ends of Greek like mosaic work, though altogether by head and shoulders and less to the purpose. And if they want hard words, they run over some worm-eaten manuscript and pick out half a dozen of the most old and obsolete to confound their reader, believing, no doubt, that they that understand their meaning will like it the better, and they that do not will admire it the more by how much the less they understand it. Nor is this way of ours of admiring what seems most foreign without its particular grace; for if there happen to be any more ambitious than others, they may give their applause with a smile, and, like the ass, shake their ears, that they may be thought to understand more than the rest of their neighbors.

But to come to the purpose: I have given you my name, but what epithet shall I add? What but that of the most foolish? For by what more proper name can so great a goddess as Folly be known to her disciples? And because it is not alike known to all from what stock I am sprung, with the Muses' good leave I'll do my endeavor to satisfy you. But yet neither the first Chaos, Orcus, Saturn, or Japhet, nor any of those threadbare, musty gods were my father, but Plutus, Riches; that only he, that is, in spite of Hesiod, Homer, nay and Jupiter himself, *Divum Pater atque Hominum Rex*, the father of gods and men, at whose single beck, as heretofore, so at present, all things sacred and profane are turned topsy-turvy. According to whose pleasure war, peace, empire, counsels, judgments, assemblies, wedlocks, bargains, leagues, laws, arts, all things light or serious—I want breath—in short, all the public and private business of mankind is governed; without whose help all that herd of gods of the poets' making, and those few of the better sort of the rest, either would not be at all, or if they were, they would be but such as live at home and keep a poor house to themselves. And to whomsoever he's an enemy, 'tis not Pallas herself that can befriend him; as on the contrary he whom he favors may lead Jupiter and his thunder in a string. This is my father and in him I glory. Nor did he produce me from his brain, as Jupiter that sour and ill-looked Pallas; but of that lovely nymph called Youth, the most beautiful and galliard of all the rest. Nor was I, like that limping blacksmith, begot in the sad and irksome bonds of matrimony. Yet, mistake me not, 'twas not that blind and decrepit Plutus in Aristophanes that got me, but such as he was in his full strength and pride of youth; and not that only, but at such a time when he had been well heated with nectar, of which he had, at one of the banquets of the gods, taken a dose extraordinary.

And as to the place of my birth, forasmuch as nowadays that is looked upon as a main point of nobility, it was neither, like Apollo's, in the floating Delos, nor Venus-like on the rolling sea, nor in any of blind Homer's as blind caves: but in the Fortunate Islands, where all things grew without plowing or sowing; where neither labor, nor old age, nor disease was ever heard of; and in whose fields neither daffodil, mallows, onions, beans, and such contemptible things would ever grow, but, on the contrary, rue, angelica, bugloss, marjoram, trefoils, roses, violets, lilies, and all the gardens of Adonis invite both your sight and your smelling. And being thus born, I did not begin the world, as other children are wont, with crying; but straight perched up and smiled on my mother. Nor do I envy to the great Jupiter the goat, his nurse, forasmuch as I was suckled by two jolly nymphs, to wit, Drunkenness, the daughter of Bacchus, and Ignorance, of Pan. And as for such my companions and followers as you perceive about me, if you have a mind to know who they are, you are not like to be the wiser for me, unless it be in Greek: this here, which you observe with that proud cast of her eye, is Φιλαυτία, Self-love; she with the smiling countenance, that is ever and anon clapping her hands, is Κολακία, Flattery; she that looks as if she were half asleep is Λήθη, Oblivion; she that sits leaning on both elbows with her hands clutched together is Μισοπονία, Laziness; she with the garland on her head, and that smells so strong of perfumes, is Ἡδονὴ, Pleasure; she with those staring eyes, moving here and there, is Ἀνοία, Madness; she with the smooth skin and full pampered body is Τρυφὴ, Wantonness; and, as to the two gods that you see with them, the one is Κῶμος, Intemperance, the other Νήγρετος ὕπνος, Dead Sleep. These, I say, are my household servants, and by their faithful counsels I have subjected all things to my dominion and erected an empire over emperors themselves. Thus have you had my lineage, education, and companions.

And now, lest I may seem to have taken upon me the name of goddess without cause, you shall in the next place understand how far my deity extends, and what advantage by it I have brought both to gods and men. For, if it was not unwisely said by somebody, that this only is to be a god, to help men; and if they are deservedly enrolled among the gods that first brought in corn and wine and such other things as are for the common good of mankind, why am not I of right the *alpha*, or first, of all the gods? who being but one, yet bestow all things on all men. For first, what is more sweet or more precious than life? And yet from whom can it more properly be said to come than from me? For neither the crab-favoured Pallas' spear nor the cloud-gathering Jupiter's shield either beget or propagate mankind; but even he himself, the father of gods and king of men at whose very beck the heavens shake, must lay by his forked thunder and those looks wherewith he conquered the giants and with which at pleasure he frightens the rest of the gods, and like a common stage player put on a disguise as often as he goes about that, which now and then he does, that is to say the getting of children: And the Stoics too, that conceive themselves next to the gods, yet show me one of them, nay the veriest bigot of the sect, and if he do not put off his beard, the badge of wisdom, though yet it be no more than what is common with him and goats; yet at least he must lay by his agree in everything. And by how much the nearer they approach to this old age, by so much they grow backward into the likeness of children, until like them they pass from life to death, without any weariness of the one, or sense of the other.

And now, let him that will compare the benefits they receive by me, the metamorphoses of the gods, of whom I shall not mention what they have done in their pettish humors but where they have been most favorable: turning one into a tree, another into a bird, a third into a grasshopper, serpent, or the like. As if there were any difference between perishing and being another thing! But I restore the same man to the best and happiest part of his life. And if men would but refrain from all commerce with wisdom and give up themselves to be governed by me, they should never know what it were to be old, but solace themselves with a perpetual youth. Do but observe our grim philosophers that are perpetually beating their brains on knotty subjects, and for the most part you'll find them grown old before they are scarcely young. And whence is it, but that their continual and restless thoughts insensibly prey upon their spirits and dry up their radical moisture? Whereas, on the contrary, my fat fools are as plump and round as a Westphalian hog, and never sensible of old age, unless perhaps, as sometimes it rarely happens, they come to be infected with wisdom, so hard a thing it is for a man to be happy in all things. And to this purpose is that no small testimony of the proverb, that says, "Folly is the only thing that keeps youth at a stay and old age afar off;" as it is verified in the Brabanders, of whom there goes this common saying, "That age, which is wont to render other men wiser, makes them the greater fools." And yet there is scarce any nation of a more jocund converse, or that is less sensible of the misery of old age, than they are. And to these, as in situation, so for manner of living, come nearest my friends the Hollanders. And why should I not call them mine, since they are so diligent observers of me that they are commonly called by my name?—of which they are so far from being ashamed, they rather pride themselves in it. Let the foolish world then be packing and seek out Medeas, Circes, Venuses, Auroras, and I know not what other fountains of restoring youth. I am sure I am the only person that both can, and have, made it good. 'Tis I alone that have that wonderful juice with which Memnon's daughter prolonged the youth of her grandfather Tithon. I am that Venus by whose favor Phaon became so young again that Sappho fell in love with him. Mine are those herbs, if yet there be any such, mine those charms, and mine that fountain that not only restores departed youth but, which is more desirable, preserves it perpetual. And if you all subscribe to this opinion, that nothing is better than youth or more execrable than age, I conceive you cannot but see how much you are indebted to me, that have retained so great a good and shut out so great an evil.

But why do I altogether spend my breath in speaking of mortals? View heaven round, and let him that will reproach me with my name if he find any one of the gods that were not stinking and contemptible were he not made acceptable by my deity. Why is it that Bacchus is always a stripling, and bushy-haired? but because he is mad, and drunk, and spends his life in drinking, dancing, revels, and May games, not having so much as the least society with Pallas. And lastly, he is so far from desiring to be accounted wise that he delights to be worshiped with sports and gambols; nor is he displeased with the proverb that gave him the surname of fool, "A greater fool than Bacchus;" which name of his was changed to Morychus, for that sitting before the gates of his temple, the wanton country people were wont to bedaub him with new wine and figs. And of scoffs, what not, have not the ancient comedies thrown on him? O foolish god, say they, and worthy to be born as you were of your father's thigh! And yet, who had not rather be your fool and sot, always merry, ever young, and making sport for other people, than either Homer's Jupiter with his crooked counsels, terrible to everyone; or old Pan with his hubbubs; or smutty Vulcan half covered with cinders; or even Pallas herself, so dreadful with her Gorgon's head and spear and a countenance like bul-beef? Why is Cupid always portrayed like a boy, but because he is a very wag and can neither do nor so much as think of anything sober? Why Venus ever in her prime, but because of her affinity with me? Witness that color of her hair, so resembling my father, from whence she is called the golden Venus; and lastly, ever laughing, if you give any credit to the poets, or their followers the statuaries. What deity did the Romans ever more religiously adore than that of Flora, the foundress of all pleasure? Nay, if you should but diligently search the lives of the most sour and morose of the gods out of Homer and the rest of the poets, you would find them all but so many pieces of Folly. And to what purpose should I run over any of the other gods' tricks when you know enough of Jupiter's loose loves? When that chaste Diana shall so far forget her sex as to be ever hunting and ready to perish for Endymion? But I had rather they should hear these things from Momus, from whom heretofore they were wont to have their shares, till in one of their angry humors they tumbled him, together with Ate, goddess of mischief, down headlong to the earth, because his wisdom, forsooth, unseasonably disturbed their happiness. Nor since that dares any mortal give him harbor, though I must confess there wanted little but that he had been received into the courts of princes, had not my companion Flattery reigned in chief there, with whom and the other there is no more correspondence than between lambs and wolves. From whence it is that the gods play the fool with the greater liberty and more content to themselves "doing all things carelessly," as says Father Homer, that is to say, without anyone to correct them. For what ridiculous stuff is seven wise men but myself, and that too for the common pleasure of mankind. The nature of all which things is such that the more of folly they have, the more they conduce to human life, which, if it were unpleasant, did not deserve the name of life; and other than such it could not well be, did not these kind of diversions wipe away tediousness, next cousin to the other.

But perhaps there are some that neglect this way of pleasure and rest satisfied in the enjoyment of their friends, calling friendship the most desirable of all things, more necessary than either air, fire, or water; so delectable that he that shall take it out of the world had as good put out the sun; and, lastly, so commendable, if yet that make anything to the matter, that neither the philosophers themselves doubted to reckon it among their chiefest good. But what if I show you that I am both the beginning and end of this so great good also? Nor shall I go about to prove it by fallacies, sorites, dilemmas, or other the like subtleties of logicians, but after my blunt way point out the thing as clearly as it were with my finger.

And now tell me if to wink, slip over, be blind at, or deceived in the vices of our friends, nay, to admire and esteem them for virtues, be not at least the next degree to folly? What is it when one kisses his mistress' freckle neck, another the wart on her nose? When a father shall swear his squint-eyed child is more lovely than Venus? What is this, I say, but mere folly? And so, perhaps you'll cry it is; and yet 'tis this only that joins friends together and continues them so joined. I speak of ordinary men, of whom none are born without their imperfections, and happy is he that is pressed with the least: for among wise princes there is either no friendship at all, or if there be, 'tis unpleasant and reserved, and that too but among a very few 'twere a crime to say none. For that the greatest part of mankind are fools, nay there is not anyone that dotes not in many things; and friendship, you know, is seldom made but among equals. And yet if it should so happen that there were a mutual good will between them, it is in no wise firm nor very long lived; that is to say, among such as are morose and more circumspect than needs, as being eagle-sighted into his friends' faults, but so blear-eyed to their own that they take not the least notice of the wallet that hangs behind their own shoulders. Since then the nature of man is such that there is scarce anyone to be found that is not subject to many errors, add to this the great diversity of minds and studies, so many slips, oversights, and chances of human life, and how is it possible there should be any true friendship between those Argus, so much as one hour, were it not for that which the Greeks excellently call ευήθειαυ? And you may render by folly or good nature, choose you whether. But what? Is not the author and parent of all our love, Cupid, as blind as a beetle? And as with him all colors agree, so from him is it that everyone likes his own sweeter-kin best, though never so ugly, and "that an old man dotes on his old wife, and a boy on his girl." These things are not only done everywhere but laughed at too; yet as ridiculous as they are, they make society pleasant, and, as it were, glue it together.

And what has been said of friendship may more reasonably be presumed of matrimony, which in truth is no other than an inseparable conjunction of life. Good God! What divorces, or what not worse than that, would daily happen were not the converse between a man and his wife supported and cherished by flattery, apishness, gentleness, ignorance, dissembling, certain retainers of mine also! Whoop holiday! how few marriages should we have, if the husband should but thoroughly examine how many tricks his pretty little mop of modesty has played before she was married! And how fewer of them would hold together, did not most of the wife's actions escape the husband's knowledge through his neglect or sottishness! And for this also you are beholden to me, by whose means it is that the husband is pleasant to his wife, the wife to her husband, and the house kept in quiet. A man is laughed at, when seeing his wife weeping he licks up her tears. But how much happier is it to be thus deceived than by being troubled with jealousy not only to torment himself but set all things in a hubbub!

In fine, I am so necessary to the making of all society and manner of life both delightful and lasting, that neither would the people long endure their governors, nor the servant his master, nor the master his footman, nor the scholar his tutor, nor one friend another, nor the wife her husband, nor the usurer the borrower, nor a soldier his commander, nor one companion another, unless all of them had their interchangeable failings, one while flattering, other while prudently conniving, and generally sweetening one another with some small relish of folly.

And now you'd think I had said all, but you shall hear yet greater things. Will he, I pray, love anyone that hates himself? Or ever agree with another who is not at peace with himself? Or beget pleasure in another that is troublesome to himself? I think no one will say it that is not more foolish than Folly. And yet, if you should exclude me, there's no man but would be so far from enduring another that he would stink in his own nostrils, be nauseated with his own actions, and himself become odious to himself; forasmuch as Nature, in too many things rather a stepdame than a parent to us, has imprinted that evil in men, especially such as have least judgment, that everyone repents him of his own condition and admires that of others. Whence it comes to pass that all her gifts, elegancy, and graces corrupt and perish. For what benefit is beauty, the greatest blessing of heaven, if it be mixed with affectation? What youth, if corrupted with the severity of old age? Lastly, what is that in the whole business of a man's life he can do with any grace to himself or others—for it is not so much a thing of art, as the very life of every action, that it be done with a good mien—unless this my friend and companion, Self-love, be present with it? Nor does she without cause supply me the place of a sister, since her whole endeavors are to act my part everywhere. For what is more foolish than for a man to study nothing else than how to please himself? To make himself the object of his own admiration? And yet, what is there that is either delightful or taking, nay rather what not the contrary, that a man does against the hair? Take away this salt of life, and the orator may even sit still with his action, the musician with all his division will be able to please no man, the player be hissed off the stage, the poet and all his Muses ridiculous, the painter with his art contemptible, and the physician with all his slip-slops go a-begging. Lastly, you will be taken for an ugly fellow instead of youthful, and a beast instead of a wise man, a child instead of eloquent, and instead of a well-bred man, a clown. So necessary a thing it is that everyone flatter himself and commend himself to himself before he can be commended by others.

Lastly, since it is the chief point of happiness "that a man is willing to be what he is," you have further abridged in this my Self-love, that no man is ashamed of his own face, no man of his own wit, no man of his own parentage, no man of his own house, no man of his manner of living, nor any man of his own country; so that a Highlander has no desire to change with an Italian, a Thracian with an Athenian, nor a Scythian for the Fortunate Islands. O the singular care of Nature, that in so great a variety of things has made all equal! Where she has been sometimes sparing of her gifts she has recompensed it with the more of self-love; though here, I must confess, I speak foolishly, it being the greatest of all other her gifts: to say nothing that no great action was ever attempted without my motion, or art brought to perfection without my help.

Is not war the very root and matter of all famed enterprises? And yet what more foolish than to undertake it for I know what trifles, especially when both parties are sure to lose more than they get by the bargain? For of those that are slain, not a word of them; and for the rest, when both sides are close engaged "and the trumpets make an ugly noise," what use of those wise men, I pray, that are so exhausted with study that their thin, cold blood has scarce any spirits left? No, it must be those blunt, fat fellows, that by how much the more they exceed in courage, fall short in understanding. Unless perhaps one had rather choose Demosthenes for a soldier, who, following the example of Archilochius, threw away his arms and betook him to his heels e'er he had scarce seen his enemy; as ill a soldier, as happy an orator.

But counsel, you'll say, is not of least concern in matters of war. In a general I grant it; but this thing of warring is not part of philosophy, but managed by parasites, panders, thieves, cut-throats, plowmen, sots, spendthrifts, and such other dregs of mankind, not philosophers; who how unapt they are even for common converse, let Socrates, whom the oracle of Apollo, though not so wisely, judged "the wisest of all men living," be witness; who stepping up to speak somewhat, I know not what, in public was forced to come down again well laughed at for his pains. Though yet in this he was not altogether a fool, that he refused the appellation of wise, and returning it back to the oracle, delivered his opinion that a wise man should abstain from meddling with public business; unless perhaps he should have rather admonished us to beware of wisdom if we intended to be reckoned among the number of men, there being nothing but his wisdom that first accused and afterwards sentenced him to the drinking of his poisoned cup. For while, as you find him in Aristophanes, philosophizing about clouds and ideas, measuring how far a flea could leap, and admiring that so small a creature as a fly should make so great a buzz, he meddled not with anything that concerned common life. But his master being in danger of his head, his scholar Plato is at hand, to wit that famous patron, that being disturbed with the noise of the people, could not go through half his first sentence. What should I speak of Theophrastus, who being about to make an oration, became as dumb as if he had met a wolf in his way, which yet would have put courage in a man of war? Or Isocrates, that was so cowhearted that he dared never attempt it? Or Tully, that great founder of the Roman eloquence, that could never begin to speak without an odd kind of trembling, like a boy that had got the hiccough; which Fabius interprets as an argument of a wise orator and one that was sensible of what he was doing; and while he says it, does he not plainly confess that wisdom is a great obstacle to the true management of business? What would become of them, think you, were they to fight it out at blows that are so dead through fear when the contest is only with empty words?

And next to these is cried up, forsooth, that goodly sentence of Plato's, "Happy is that commonwealth where a philosopher is prince, or whose prince is addicted to philosophy." When yet if you consult historians, you'll find no princes more pestilent to the commonwealth than where the empire has fallen to some smatterer in philosophy or one given to letters. To the truth of which I think the Catoes give sufficient credit; of whom the one was ever disturbing the peace of the commonwealth with his hair-brained accusations; the other, while he too wisely vindicated its liberty, quite overthrew it. Add to this the Bruti, Casii, nay Cicero himself, that was no less pernicious to the commonwealth of Rome than was Demosthenes to that of Athens. Besides M. Antoninus (that I may give you one instance that there was once one good emperor; for with much ado I can make it out) was become burdensome and hated of his subjects upon no other score but that he was so great a philosopher. But admitting him good, he did the commonwealth more hurt in leaving behind him such a son as he did

like Alcibiades' Sileni or rural gods, carry a double face, but not the
least alike; so that what at first sight seems to be death, if you view it
narrowly may prove to be life; and so the contrary. What appears
beautiful may chance to be deformed; what wealthy, a very beggar;
what infamous, praiseworthy; what learned, a dunce; what lusty, feeble;
what jocund, sad; what noble, base; what lucky, unfortunate; what
friendly, an enemy; and what healthful, noisome. In short, view the
inside of these Sileni, and you'll find them quite other than what they
appear; which, if perhaps it shall not seem so philosophically spoken,
I'll make it plain to you "after my blunt way." Who would not conceive
a prince a great lord and abundant in everything? But yet being so ill-
furnished with the gifts of the mind, and ever thinking he shall never
have enough, he's the poorest of all men. And then for his mind so
given up to vice, 'tis a shame how it enslaves him. I might in like
manner philosophize of the rest; but let this one, for example's sake, be
enough.

Yet why this? will someone say. Have patience, and I'll show you
what I drive at. If anyone seeing a player acting his part on a stage
should go about to strip him of his disguise and show him to the people
in his true native form, would he not, think you, not only spoil the
whole design of the play, but deserve himself to be pelted off with
stones as a phantastical fool and one out of his wits? But nothing is
more common with them than such changes; the same person one while
impersonating a woman, and another while a man; now a youngster,
and by and by a grim seignior; now a king, and presently a peasant;
now a god, and in a trice again an ordinary fellow. But to discover this
were to spoil all, it being the only thing that entertains the eyes of the
spectators. And what is all this life but a kind of comedy, wherein men
walk up and down in one another's disguises and act their respective
parts, till the property-man brings them back to the attiring house. And
yet he often orders a different dress, and makes him that came but just
now off in the robes of a king put on the rags of a beggar. Thus are all
things represented by counterfeit, and yet without this there was no
living.

And here if any wise man, as it were dropped from heaven, should
start up and cry, this great thing whom the world looks upon for a god
and I know not what is not so much as a man, for that like a beast he is
led by his passions, but the worst of slaves, inasmuch as he gives
himself up willingly to so many and such detestable masters. Again if
he should bid a man that were bewailing the death of his father to
laugh, for that he now began to live by having got an estate, without
which life is but a kind of death; or call another that were boasting of
his family ill begotten or base, because he is so far removed from virtue
that is the only fountain of nobility; and so of the rest: what else would
he get by it but be thought himself mad and frantic? For as nothing is

more foolish than preposterous wisdom, so nothing is more unadvised than a forward unseasonable prudence. And such is his that does not comply with the present time "and order himself as the market goes," but forgetting that law of feasts, "either drink or begone," undertakes to disprove a common received opinion. Whereas on the contrary 'tis the part of a truly prudent man not to be wise beyond his condition, but either to take no notice of what the world does, or run with it for company. But this is foolish, you'll say; nor shall I deny it, provided always you be so civil on the other side as to confess that this is to act a part in that world.

But, O you gods, "shall I speak or hold my tongue?" But why should I be silent in a thing that is more true than truth itself? However it might not be amiss perhaps in so great an affair to call forth the Muses from Helicon, since the poets so often invoke them upon every foolish occasion. Be present then awhile, and assist me, you daughters of Jupiter, while I make it out that there is no way to that so much famed wisdom, nor access to that fortress as they call it of happiness, but under the banner of Folly. And first 'tis agreed of all hands that our passions belong to Folly; inasmuch as we judge a wise man from a fool by this, that the one is ordered by them, the other by reason; and therefore the Stoics remove from a wise man all disturbances of mind as so many diseases. But these passions do not only the office of a tutor to such as are making towards the port of wisdom, but are in every exercise of virtue as it were spurs and incentives, nay and encouragers to well doing: which though that great Stoic Seneca most strongly denies, and takes from a wise man all affections whatever, yet in doing that he leaves him not so much as a man but rather a new kind of god that was never yet nor ever like to be. Nay, to speak plainer, he sets up a stony semblance of a man, void of all sense and common feeling of humanity. And much good to them with this wise man of theirs; let them enjoy him to themselves, love him without competitors, and live with him in Plato's commonwealth, the country of ideas, or Tantalus' orchards. For who would not shun and startle at such a man, as at some unnatural accident or spirit? A man dead to all sense of nature and common affections, and no more moved with love or pity than if he were a flint or rock; whose censure nothing escapes; that commits no errors himself, but has a lynx's eyes upon others; measures everything by an exact line, and forgives nothing; pleases himself with himself only; the only rich, the only wise, the only free man, and only king; in brief, the only man that is everything, but in his own single judgment only; that cares not for the friendship of any man, being himself a friend to no man; makes no doubt to make the gods stoop to him, and condemns and laughs at the whole actions of our life? And yet such a beast is this their perfect wise man. But tell me pray, if the thing were to be carried by most voices, what city would choose him for its manner should those logicians have done and distinguished madness from madness, if at least they would be thought to be well in their wits themselves. For all madness is not miserable, or Horace had never called his poetical fury a beloved madness; nor Plato placed the raptures of poets, prophets, and lovers among the chiefest blessings of this life; nor that sibyl in Virgil called Aeneas' travels mad labors. But there are two sorts of madness, the one that which the revengeful Furies send privily from hell, as often as they let loose their snakes and put into men's breasts either the desire of war, or an insatiate thirst after gold, or some dishonest love, or parricide, or incest, or sacrilege, or the like plagues, or when they terrify some guilty soul with the conscience of his crimes; the other, but nothing like this, that which comes from me and is of all other things the most desirable; which happens as often as some pleasing dotage not only clears the mind of its troublesome cares but renders it more jocund. And this was that which, as a special blessing of the gods, Cicero, writing to his friend Atticus, wished to himself, that he might be the less sensible of those miseries that then hung over the commonwealth.

Nor was that Grecian in Horace much wide of it, who was so far made that he would sit by himself whole days in the theatre laughing and clapping his hands, as if he had seen some tragedy acting, whereas in truth there was nothing presented; yet in other things a man well enough, pleasant among his friends, kind to his wife, and so good a master to his servants that if they had broken the seal of his bottle, he would not have run mad for it. But at last, when by the care of his friends and physic he was freed from his distemper and become his own man again, he thus expostulates with them, "Now, by Pollux, my friends, you have rather killed than preserved me in thus forcing me from my pleasure." By which you see he liked it so well that he lost it against his will. And trust me, I think they were the madder of the two, and had the greater need of hellebore, that should offer to look upon so pleasant a madness as an evil to be removed by physic; though yet I have not determined whether every distemper of the sense or understanding be to be called madness.

For neither he that having weak eyes should take a mule for an ass, nor he that should admire an insipid poem as excellent would be presently thought mad; but he that not only errs in his senses but is deceived also in his judgment, and that too more than ordinary and upon all occasions,—he, I must confess, would be thought to come very near to it. As if anyone hearing an ass bray should take it for excellent music, or a beggar conceive himself a king. And yet this kind of madness, if, as it commonly happens, it turn to pleasure, it brings a great delight not only to them that are possessed with it but to those also that behold it, though perhaps they may not be altogether so mad as the other, for the species of this madness is much larger than the people take it to be. For one mad man laughs at another, and beget themselves a mutual pleasure. Nor does it seldom happen that he that is the more mad, laughs at him that is less mad. And in this every man is the more happy in how many respects the more he is mad; and if I were judge in the case, he should be ranged in that class of folly that is peculiarly mine, which in truth is so large and universal that I scarce know anyone in all mankind that is wise at all hours, or has not some tang or other of madness.

And to this class do they appertain that slight everything in comparison of hunting and protest they take an unimaginable pleasure to hear the yell of the horns and the yelps of the hounds, and I believe could pick somewhat extraordinary out of their very excrement. And then what pleasure they take to see a buck or the like unlaced? Let ordinary fellows cut up an ox or a weather, 'twere a crime to have this done by anything less than a gentleman! who with his hat off, on his bare knees, and a cuttoe for that purpose (for every sword or knife is not allowable), with a curious superstition and certain postures, lays open the several parts in their respective order; while they that hem him in admire it with silence, as some new religious ceremony, though perhaps they have seen it a hundred times before. And if any of them chance to get the least piece of it, he presently thinks himself no small gentleman. In all which they drive at nothing more than to become beasts themselves, while yet they imagine they live the life of princes.

And next these may be reckoned those that have such an itch of building; one while changing rounds into squares, and presently again squares into rounds, never knowing either measure or end, till at last, reduced to the utmost poverty, there remains not to them so much as a place where they may lay their head, or wherewith to fill their bellies. And why all this? but that they may pass over a few years in feeding their foolish fancies.

And, in my opinion, next these may be reckoned such as with their new inventions and occult arts undertake to change the forms of things and hunt all about after a certain fifth essence; men so bewitched with this present hope that it never repents them of their pains or expense, but are ever contriving how they may cheat themselves, till, having spent all, there is not enough left them to provide another furnace. And yet they have not done dreaming these their pleasant dreams but encourage others, as much as in them lies, to the same happiness. And at last, when they are quite lost in all their expectations, they cheer up themselves with this sentence, "In great things the very attempt is enough," and then complain of the shortness of man's life that is not sufficient for so great an understanding.

And then for gamesters, I am a little doubtful whether they are to be admitted into our college; and yet 'tis a foolish and ridiculous sight to see some addicted so to it that they can no sooner hear the rattling of should this wise man chat to the people, from what happiness into how great troubles would he draw them?

Of this college also are they who in their lifetime appoint with what solemnity they'll be buried, and particularly set down how many torches, how many mourners, how many singers, how many almsmen they will have at it; as if any sense of it could come to them, or that it were a shame to them that their corpse were not honorably interred; so curious are they herein, as if, like the Ædiles of old, these were to present some shows or banquet to the people.

And though I am in haste, yet I cannot yet pass by them who, though they differ nothing from the meanest cobbler, yet 'tis scarcely credible how they flatter themselves with the empty title of nobility. One derives his pedigree from Aeneas, another from Brutus, a third from the star by the tail of Ursa Major. They show you on every side the statues and pictures of their ancestors; run over their great-grandfathers and the great-great-grandfathers of both lines, and the ancient matches of their families, when themselves yet are but once removed from a statue, if not worse than those trifles they boast of. And yet by means of this pleasant self-love they live a happy life. Nor are they less fools who admire these beasts as if they were gods.

But what do I speak of any one or the other particular kind of men, as if this self-love had not the same effect everywhere and rendered most men superabundantly happy? As when a fellow, more deformed than a baboon, shall believe himself handsomer than Homer's Nireus. Another, as soon as he can draw two or three lines with a compass, presently thinks himself a Euclid. A third, that understands music no more than my horse, and for his voice as hoarse as a dunghill cock, shall yet conceive himself another Hermogenes. But of all madness that's the most pleasant when a man, seeing another any way excellent in what he pretends to himself, makes his boasts of it as confidently as if it were his own. And such was that rich fellow in Seneca, who whenever he told a story had his servants at his elbow to prompt him the names; and to that height had they flattered him that he did not question but he might venture a rubber at cuffs, a man otherwise so weak he could scarce stand, only presuming on this, that he had a company of sturdy servants about him.

Or to what purpose is it I should mind you of our professors of arts? Forasmuch as this self-love is so natural to them all that they had rather part with their father's land than their foolish opinions; but chiefly players, fiddlers, orators, and poets, of which the more ignorant each of them is, the more insolently he pleases himself, that is to say vaunts and spreads out his plumes. And like lips find like lettuce; nay, the more foolish anything is, the more 'tis admired, the greater number being ever tickled at the worst things, because, as I said before, most men are so subject to folly. And therefore if the more foolish a man is, the more he pleases himself and is admired by others, to what purpose should he beat his brains about true knowledge, which first will cost him dear, and next render him the more troublesome and less confident, and lastly, please only a few?

And now I consider it, Nature has planted, not only in particular men but even in every nation, and scarce any city is there without it, a kind of common self-love. And hence is it that the English, besides other things, particularly challenge to themselves beauty, music, and feasting. The Scots are proud of their nobility, alliance to the crown, and logical subtleties. The French think themselves the only well-bred men. The Parisians, excluding all others, arrogate to themselves the only knowledge of divinity. The Italians affirm they are the only masters of good letters and eloquence, and flatter themselves on this account, that of all others they only are not barbarous. In which kind of happiness those of Rome claim the first place, still dreaming to themselves of somewhat, I know not what, of old Rome. The Venetians fancy themselves happy in the opinion of their nobility. The Greeks, as if they were the only authors of sciences, swell themselves with the titles of the ancient heroes. The Turk, and all that sink of the truly barbarous, challenge to themselves the only glory of religion and laugh at Christians as superstitious. And much more pleasantly the Jews expect to this day the coming of the Messiah, and so obstinately contend for their Law of Moses. The Spaniards give place to none in the reputation of soldiery. The Germans pride themselves in their tallness of stature and skill in magic.

And, not to instance in every particular, you see, I conceive, how much satisfaction this Self-love, who has a sister also not unlike herself called Flattery, begets everywhere; for self-love is no more than the soothing of a man's self, which, done to another, is flattery. And though perhaps at this day it may be thought infamous, yet it is so only with them that are more taken with words than things. They think truth is inconsistent with flattery, but that it is much otherwise we may learn from the examples of true beasts. What more fawning than a dog? And yet what more trusty? What has more of those little tricks than a squirrel? And yet what more loving to man? Unless, perhaps you'll say, men had better converse with fierce lions, merciless tigers, and furious leopards. For that flattery is the most pernicious of all things, by means of which some treacherous persons and mockers have run the credulous into such mischief. But this of mine proceeds from a certain gentleness and uprightness of mind and comes nearer to virtue than its opposite, austerity, or a morose and troublesome peevishness, as Horace calls it. This supports the dejected, relieves the distressed, encourages the fainting, awakens the stupid, refreshes the sick, supplies the untractable, joins loves together, and keeps them so joined. It entices children to take their learning, makes old men frolic, and, under the

God the Father hates the Son; or whether it was possible that Christ
could have taken upon Him the likeness of a woman, or of the devil, or
of an ass, or of a stone, or of a gourd; and then how that gourd should
have preached, wrought miracles, or been hung on the cross; and what
Peter had consecrated if he had administered the Sacrament at what
time the body of Christ hung upon the cross; or whether at the same
time he might be said to be man; whether after the Resurrection there
will be any eating and drinking, since we are so much afraid of hunger
and thirst in this world. There are infinite of these subtle trifles, and
others more subtle than these, of notions, relations, instants, formalities,
quiddities, haecceities, which no one can perceive without a Lynceus
whose eyes could look through a stone wall and discover those things
through the thickest darkness that never were.

Add to this those their other determinations, and those too so
contrary to common opinion that those oracles of the Stoics, which they
call paradoxes, seem in comparison of these but blockish and idle—as
'tis a lesser crime to kill a thousand men than to set a stitch on a poor
man's shoe on the Sabbath day; and that a man should rather choose
that the whole world with all food and raiment, as they say, should
perish, than tell a lie, though never so inconsiderable. And these most
subtle subtleties are rendered yet more subtle by the several methods of
so many Schoolmen, that one might sooner wind himself out of a
labyrinth than the entanglements of the realists, nominalists, Thomists,
Albertists, Occamists, Scotists. Nor have I named all the several sects,
but only some of the chief; in all which there is so much doctrine and
so much difficulty that I may well conceive the apostles, had they been
to deal with these new kind of divines, had needed to have prayed in
aid of some other spirit.

Paul knew what faith was, and yet when he said, "Faith is the
substance of things hoped for, and the evidence of things not seen," he
did not define it doctor-like. And as he understood charity well himself,
so he did as illogically divide and define it to others in his first Epistle
to the Corinthians, Chapter the thirteenth. And devoutly, no doubt, did
the apostles consecrate the Eucharist; yet, had they been asked the
question touching the "terminus a quo" and the "terminus ad quem" of
transubstantiation; of the manner how the same body can be in several
places at one and the same time; of the difference the body of Christ
has in heaven from that of the cross, or this in the Sacrament; in what
point of time transubstantiation is, whereas prayer, by means of which
it is, as being a discrete quantity, is transient; they would not, I
conceive, have answered with the same subtlety as the Scotists dispute
and define it. They knew the mother of Jesus, but which of them has so
philosophically demonstrated how she was preserved from original sin
as have done our divines? Peter received the keys, and from Him too
that would not have trusted them with a person unworthy; yet whether

he had understanding or no, I know not, for certainly he never attained to that subtlety to determine how he could have the key of knowledge that had no knowledge himself. They baptized far and near, and yet taught nowhere what was the formal, material, efficient, and final cause of baptism, nor made the least mention of delible and indelible characters. They worshiped, 'tis true, but in spirit, following herein no other than that of the Gospel, "God is a Spirit, and they that worship, must worship him in spirit and truth;" yet it does not appear it was at that time revealed to them that an image sketched on the wall with a coal was to be worshiped with the same worship as Christ Himself, if at least the two forefingers be stretched out, the hair long and uncut, and have three rays about the crown of the head. For who can conceive these things, unless he has spent at least six and thirty years in the philosophical and supercoelestial whims of Aristotle and the Schoolmen?

In like manner, the apostles press to us grace; but which of them distinguishes between free grace and grace that makes a man acceptable? They exhort us to good works, and yet determine not what is the work working, and what a resting in the work done. They incite us to charity, and yet make no difference between charity infused and charity wrought in us by our own endeavors. Nor do they declare whether it be an accident or a substance, a thing created or uncreated. They detest and abominate sin, but let me not live if they could define according to art what that is which we call sin, unless perhaps they were inspired by the spirit of the Scotists. Nor can I be brought to believe that Paul, by whose learning you may judge the rest, would have so often condemned questions, disputes, genealogies, and, as himself calls them, "strifes of words," if he had thoroughly understood those subtleties, especially when all the debates and controversies of those times were rude and blockish in comparison of the more than Chrysippean subtleties of our masters. Although yet the gentlemen are so modest that if they meet with anything written by the apostles not so smooth and even as might be expected from a master, they do not presently condemn it but handsomely bend it to their own purpose, so great respect and honor do they give, partly to antiquity and partly to the name of apostle. And truly 'twas a kind of injustice to require so great things of them that never heard the least word from their masters concerning it. And so if the like happen in Chrysostom, Basil, Jerome, they think it enough to say they are not obliged by it.

The apostles also confuted the heathen philosophers and Jews, a people than whom none more obstinate, but rather by their good lives and miracles than syllogisms: and yet there was scarce one among them that was capable of understanding the least "quodlibet" of the Scotists. But now, where is that heathen or heretic that must not presently stoop to such wire-drawn subtleties, unless he be so thick-skulled that he impudence, they represent to us, for so they call it, the lives of the apostles. Yet what is more pleasant than that they do all things by rule and, as it were, a kind of mathematics, the least swerving from which were a crime beyond forgiveness—as how many knots their shoes must be tied with, of what color everything is, what distinction of habits, of what stuff made, how many straws broad their girdles and of what fashion, how many bushels wide their cowl, how many fingers long their hair, and how many hours sleep; which exact equality, how disproportionate it is, among such variety of bodies and tempers, who is there that does not perceive it? And yet by reason of these fooleries they not only set slight by others, but each different order, men otherwise professing apostolical charity, despise one another, and for the different wearing of a habit, or that 'tis of darker color, they put all things in combustion. And among these there are some so rigidly religious that their upper garment is haircloth, their inner of the finest linen; and, on the contrary, others wear linen without and hair next their skins. Others, again, are as afraid to touch money as poison, and yet neither forbear wine nor dallying with women. In a word, 'tis their only care that none of them come near one another in their manner of living, nor do they endeavor how they may be like Christ, but how they may differ among themselves.

And another great happiness they conceive in their names, while they call themselves Cordiliers, and among these too, some are Colletes, some Minors, some Minims, some Crossed; and again, these are Benedictines, those Bernardines; these Carmelites, those Augustines; these Williamites, and those Jacobines; as if it were not worth the while to be called Christians. And of these, a great part build so much on their ceremonies and petty traditions of men that they think one heaven is too poor a reward for so great merit, little dreaming that the time will come when Christ, not regarding any of these trifles, will call them to account for His precept of charity. One shall show you a large trough full of all kinds of fish; another tumble you out so many bushels of prayers; another reckon you so many myriads of fasts, and fetch them up again in one dinner by eating till he cracks again; another produces more bundles of ceremonies than seven of the stoutest ships would be able to carry; another brags he has not touched a penny these three score years without two pair of gloves at least upon his hands; another wears a cowl so lined with grease that the poorest tarpaulin would not stoop to take it up; another will tell you he has lived these fifty-five years like a sponge, continually fastened to the same place; another is grown hoarse with his daily chanting; another has contracted a lethargy by his solitary living; and another the palsy in his tongue for want of speaking. But Christ, interrupting them in their vanities, which otherwise were endless, will ask them, "Whence this new kind of Jews? I acknowledge one commandment, which is truly mine, of which alone

I hear nothing. I promised, 'tis true, my Father's heritage, and that without parables, not to cowls, odd prayers, and fastings, but to the duties of faith and charity. Nor can I acknowledge them that least acknowledge their faults. They that would seem holier than myself, let them if they like possess to themselves those three hundred sixty-five heavens of Basilides the heretic's invention, or command them whose foolish traditions they have preferred before my precepts to erect them a new one." When they shall hear these things and see common ordinary persons preferred before them, with what countenance, think you, will they behold one another? In the meantime they are happy in their hopes, and for this also they are beholding to me.

And yet these kind of people, though they are as it were of another commonwealth, no man dares despise, especially those begging friars, because they are privy to all men's secrets by means of confessions, as they call them. Which yet were no less than treason to discover, unless, being got drunk, they have a mind to be pleasant, and then all comes out, that is to say by hints and conjectures but suppressing the names. But if anyone should anger these wasps, they'll sufficiently revenge themselves in their public sermons and so point out their enemy by circumlocutions that there's no one but understands whom 'tis they mean, unless he understand nothing at all; nor will they give over their barking till you throw the dogs a bone. And now tell me, what juggler or mountebank you had rather behold than hear them rhetorically play the fool in their preachments, and yet most sweetly imitating what rhetoricians have written touching the art of good speaking? Good God! what several postures they have! How they shift their voice, sing out their words, skip up and down, and are ever and anon making such new faces that they confound all things with noise! And yet this knack of theirs is no less a mystery that runs in succession from one brother to another; which though it be not lawful for me to know, however I'll venture at it by conjectures. And first they invoke whatever they have scraped from the poets; and in the next place, if they are to discourse of charity, they take their rise from the river Nilus; or to set out the mystery of the cross, from bell and the dragon; or to dispute of fasting, from the twelve signs of the zodiac; or, being to preach of faith, ground their matter on the square of a circle.

I have heard myself one, and he no small fool—I was mistaken, I would have said scholar—that being in a famous assembly explaining the mystery of the Trinity, that he might both let them see his learning was not ordinary and withal satisfy some theological ears, he took a new way, to wit from the letters, syllables, and the word itself; then from the coherence of the nominative case and the verb, and the adjective and substantive: and while most of the audience wondered, and some of them muttered that of Horace, "What does all this trumpery drive at?" at last he brought the matter to this head, that he agreement with Christ; and yet, omitting all the other, they make this their only business. Here you'll see decrepit old fellows acting the parts of young men, neither troubled at their costs, nor wearied with their labors, nor discouraged at anything, so they may have the liberty of turning laws, religion, peace, and all things else quite topsy-turvy. Nor are they destitute of their learned flatterers that call that palpable madness zeal, piety, and valor, having found out a new way by which a man may kill his brother without the least breach of that charity which, by the command of Christ, one Christian owes another. And here, in troth, I'm a little at a stand whether the ecclesiastical German electors gave them this example, or rather took it from them; who, laying aside their habit, benedictions, and all the like ceremonies, so act the part of commanders that they think it a mean thing, and least beseeming a bishop, to show the least courage to God-ward unless it be in a battle.

And as to the common herd of priests, they account it a crime to degenerate from the sanctity of their prelates. Heidah! How soldier-like they bustle about the *jus divinum* of titles, and how quick-sighted they are to pick the least thing out of the writings of the ancients wherewith they may fright the common people and convince them, if possible, that more than a tenth is due! Yet in the meantime it least comes in their heads how many things are everywhere extant concerning that duty which they owe the people. Nor does their shorn crown in the least admonish them that a priest should be free from all worldly desires and think of nothing but heavenly things. Whereas on the contrary, these jolly fellows say they have sufficiently discharged their offices if they but anyhow mumble over a few odd prayers, which, so help me, Hercules! I wonder if any god either hear or understand, since they do neither themselves, especially when they thunder them out in that manner they are wont. But this they have in common with those of the heathens, that they are vigilant enough to the harvest of their profit, nor is there any of them that is not better read in those laws than the Scripture. Whereas if there be anything burdensome, they prudently lay that on other men's shoulders and shift it from one to the other, as men toss a ball from hand to hand, following herein the example of lay princes who commit the government of their kingdoms to their grand ministers, and they again to others, and leave all study of piety to the common people. In like manner the common people put it over to those they call ecclesiastics, as if themselves were no part of the Church, or that their vow in baptism had lost its obligation. Again, the priests that call themselves secular, as if they were initiated to the world, not to Christ, lay the burden on the regulars; the regulars on the monks; the monks that have more liberty on those that have less; and all of them on the mendicants; the mendicants on the Carthusians, among whom, if anywhere, this piety lies buried, but yet so close that scarce anyone can perceive it. In like manner the popes, the most diligent of all others in gathering in the harvest of money, refer all their apostolical work to the bishops, the bishops to the parsons, the parsons to the vicars, the vicars to their brother mendicants, and they again throw back the care of the flock on those that take the wool.

But it is not my business to sift too narrowly the lives of prelates and priests for fear I seem to have intended rather a satire than an oration, and be thought to tax good princes while I praise the bad. And therefore, what I slightly taught before has been to no other end but that it might appear that there's no man can live pleasantly unless he be initiated to my rites and have me propitious to him. For how can it be otherwise when Fortune, the great directress of all human affairs, and myself are so all one that she was always an enemy to those wise men, and on the contrary so favorable to fools and careless fellows that all things hit luckily to them?

You have heard of that Timotheus, the most fortunate general of the Athenians, of whom came that proverb, "His net caught fish, though he were asleep;" and that "The owl flies;" whereas these others hit properly, wise men "born in the fourth month;" and again, "He rides Sejanus's his horse;" and "gold of Toulouse," signifying thereby the extremity of ill fortune. But I forbear the further threading of proverbs, lest I seem to have pilfered my friend Erasmus' adages. Fortune loves those that have least wit and most confidence and such as like that saying of Caesar, "The die is thrown." But wisdom makes men bashful, which is the reason that those wise men have so little to do, unless it be with poverty, hunger, and chimney corners; that they live such neglected, unknown, and hated lives: whereas fools abound in money, have the chief commands in the commonwealth, and in a word, flourish every way. For if it be happiness to please princes and to be conversant among those golden and diamond gods, what is more unprofitable than wisdom, or what is it these kind of men have, may more justly be censured? If wealth is to be got, how little good at it is that merchant like to do, if following the precepts of wisdom, he should boggle at perjury; or being taken in a lie, blush; or in the least regard the sad scruples of those wise men touching rapine and usury. Again, if a man sue for honors or church preferments, an ass or wild ox shall sooner get them than a wise man. If a man's in love with a young wench, none of the least humors in this comedy, they are wholly addicted to fools and are afraid of a wise man and fly him as they would a scorpion. Lastly, whoever intend to live merry and frolic, shut their doors against wise men and admit anything sooner. In brief, go whither you will, among prelates, princes, judges, magistrates, friends, enemies, from highest to lowest, and you'll find all things done by money; which, as a wise man condemns it, so it takes a special care not to come near him. What shall I say? There is no measure or end of my praises, and yet 'tis fit my oration have an end. And therefore I'll even break off; and yet, before I

Printed in Great Britain
by Amazon